Cantes flamencos

Cantes Flamencos

The Deep Songs of Spain

Introduced & translated by

Michael Smith & Luis Ingelmo

Shearsman Books

Published in 2012 in the United Kingdom by
Shearsman Books Ltd.,
50 Westons Hill Drive,
Emersons Green
Bristol
BS16 7DF

Shearsman Books Ltd Registered Office
30–31 St. James Place, Mangotsfield, Bristol BS16 9JB
(this address not for correspondence)

www.shearsman.com

ISBN 978-1-84861-210-5

Acknowledgements
Earlier versions of these translations appeared in *Maldon & Other
Translations* by Michael Smith (Exeter: Shearsman Books, 2004).

'Sorpresa' (Surprise) by Federico García Lorca © Herederos de
Federico García Lorca from *Obras Completas* (Galaxia Gutenberg,
1996 edition). Translation by Michael Smith © Herederos de
Federico García Lorca and Michael Smith. All rights reserved.

Extract from *A Rose for Winter* by Laurie Lee reprinted by
permission of PFD on behalf of the Estate of Laurie Lee,
copyright © 1955 by Laurie Lee.

Cantes Flamencos

Classification of *cantes flamencos*

In Federico García Lorca's famous talk, *Cante jondo (Primitivo canto andaluz)*, given on February 19, 1922, the great Andalusian poet stated his belief, supported by his friend the composer Manuel de Falla, that the *cante jondo* had very deep roots in Spanish culture, that it drew on Eastern sources, that it was sung without musical accompaniment and that it is the purest form of folksong; the *flamenco*, on the other hand, he asserted, came into existence in the 18th century, was accompanied by guitar and dance and, despite its charm, could be said to constitute a dilution of the *cante jondo*, being primarily entertainment whereas the *cante jondo* was a deep cry from the soul.

Disagreeing with Lorca and Falla, Félix Grande, probably the most famous contemporary *flamencoist*, believes that there are two principal categories in what are generically called *cantes flamencos* and he summaries these as follows:

Cante Grande

Tonás (from which developed *martinetes*, *deblas*, *carceleras*): These usually have four lines of eight syllables rhyming assonantly a-b-c-b. Originally they were sung without musical accompaniment.

Polo: This is earlier than the *toná* and became popular after the *toná* emerged.

Siguiriya: This has the packed emotion of the *toná*. It was originally sung without musical accompaniment and it has a different metrical structure from the *toná*.

Soleá: This can have three or four lines of eight syllables. It is sung in different ways and is not derived from the *siguiriya* as Lorca believed.

Saeta: This is a solemn song for religious occasions.

Cante Chico

This category includes the *tango* (not the Argentine one), *bulería*, *fandango* and some others. They are usually happy songs with guitar accompaniment. They are most people's notion of *flamenco*. They are primarily entertainment.

Grande finds support for this classification in the writings of Antonio Machado y Álvarez who used the pseudonym "Demófilo" and was the father of the great poet Antonio Machado and his brother Manuel. "Demófilo's" two seminal collections are *Colección de cantes flamencos* (Seville, 1881) and *Cantes flamencos y cantares* (Madrid, 1887). In introducing his compilations "Demófilo" says that he believes that the categories insisted on by the *cantadores* from whom he collected his material had more to do with musical inflections than with anything else, but he nonetheless accommodated their insistence out of respect for them.

"Demófilo" noted the peculiarity of *flamenco* as a poetic-musical genre which was neither folkloric nor the property of all the people but the preserve of a limited group of *cantaores* and devotees of the *cante*:

> *Cantes flamencos* constitute a poetic genre predominantly lyrical, which is, in our judgement, the least popular of all the so-called popular songs; it is a genre peculiar to the *cantadores* … The people, with the exception of the *cantadores* and their followers whom we would call *diletantti* in the context of opera, are ignorant of these *coplas*, do not know how to sing them and many have not even heard them.

> *Los cantes flamencos constituyen un género predominantemente lírico, que es, a nuestro juicio, el menos popular de todos los llamados populares; es un género proprio de cantadores […] El pueblo, a excepción de los cantadores y aficionados, a los que llamaríamos diletantti, si se tratara de óperas, desconoce estas coplas, no sabe cantarlas, y muchas de ellas ni aun las ha escuchado.*

Comparing the non-folkloric character of the *cantes flamencos* with simply popular *coplas*, he noted of the *cantes* that

> The words of these compositions are generally very sad and embrace at times very deep and subtle emotions and images that reveal extraordinary strength of imagination.

> The subject matter of these *coplas* is almost invariably personal emotion and misfortune.

> ... for every thousand *flamenco* compositions ... there are twenty thousand Andalusian ones.

> *La letra de estas composiciones es, por lo común, tristísima y encierra a veces sentimientos muy profundos y delicados e imágenes que revelan extraordinario vigor de fantasía.*

> *Los asuntos de estas coplas son casi siempre motivos o desgracias personales.*

> *[...] por cada mil composiciones flamencas [...] hay veinte mil andaluzas.*

"Demófilo" identified the flamenco with the gypsies. "The gypsies," he wrote, "call the Andalusians *gachós*, and these call the gypsies *flamencos*." His summing up of this relationship between the popular and the gypsy is worth quoting:

> The gypsy *cantes* ... Andalusianising themselves, so to speak, or becoming *gachonales* ... will gradually continue to lose their primitive character and orig-inality and will become a mixed genre, which will continue to bear the name of *flamenco* as a synonym for gypsy but which will be basically a confused mixture of heterogeneous elements.

> *Los cantes gitanos [...], andaluzándose, si cabe esta palabra, o haciéndoselo gachonales [...] irán perdiendo poco a poco su primitivo carácter y originalidad y se convertirán en un género mixto, al que se seguirá dando el nombre de flamenco,*

9

como sinónimo de gitano, pero que será en el fondo una
mezcla confusa de elementos muy heterogéneos.

As regards the question of why the word *flamenco* was used of the gypsies, a question still entrenched in scholarly debate, we may be permitted a personal note. Many years ago while living in a remote village in Ávila Michael Smith heard the villagers speaking excitedly of a visit to the village of a small circus. Almost all the people of the circus were gypsies and yet the villagers always referred to them as *húngaros* as if for them that word was a synonym for gypsies. Could it be that the gypsies who came with Spaniards returning from the Low Lands were called Flemings because of their identification with that region?

As it is the purpose of the present collection to convey to the reader without Spanish something of the *literary* value of *cantes flamencos* we have not bothered with any complex system of classification and have settled for leaving them all under the generic title of *cantes flamencos* although almost all of them are what Lorca understood by *cante jondo*. Readers who wish to know more about the technicalities of *flamenco* can consult Félix Grande's book, *Memoria del flamenco* (Madrid: Alianza Editorial, 1999).

Words Without Music?

An important question to be confronted in putting these brief lyrics into English is whether they can survive, with any worthwhile value, their separation from the whole guitar and dance ambience in which they become truly what they are. Our answer to that is we think something worthwhile does survive. We mean this in the sense that we can say that something worthwhile of a play can be appreciated apart from the play in its theatrical production. There is a *literary* quality in many of these *cantes* (not by any means in all) which can be carried over into English. That literary quality is produced by the demands of the total genre, by the compression the genre demands, by the need for the lyrics to carry the weight of the performance.

Let us take an example:

> *I am not who I was*
> *nor what I used to be;*
> *I'm a sad piece of furniture*
> *put away at the wall.*

The first line hints that things were not always so. The speaker was once estimable, whether by lover or, more generally, socially. The imperfect tense of the second line subtly rejects any dogmatic assertiveness or self-righteousness. There is no sense of anger at the abandonment. Perhaps it is the speaker's own fault that he was abandoned. The metaphor of the piece of furniture conveys a sense of obsolescence. The item of furniture has outlived its usefulness; it is not the pristine thing it once was. Yet it is not dumped out, disposed of. It still has a presence though discarded from use. There is a real poignancy in that lingering presence, as of a haunting ghost still present at the scene of its corporeal demise.

We do not think we are reading too much out of these four lines. Further narratives could be elicited. What matters, what is of literary value is the care with which the evocation has been constructed, the choice of language and the choice of metaphor. That said, it would be wrong to give the impression that what is offered here is an attempt to communicate the experience of listening to a good *flamenco* performance. The music and the singer are indispensable to that. Still, these lyrics in English have something to offer. And we have not attempted to dress them up in any way: that would have been a double betrayal. We have tried to be highly selective in our choices. Only some of them work in English, and there is a great deal of repetition in the corpus that had to be avoided.

Finally, despite the often quoted statement from Robert Frost that poetry is what is lost in translation, we take some comfort from the words of the great Chilean poet, Vicente Huidobro: "It is difficult and even impossible;" writes Huidobro in his poetic manifesto, *El creacionismo*, "to translate a poetry in which the importance of other elements dominates. You cannot translate the music of the words, the rhythms of the verses which vary from one language to another; but when the importance of the poem resides above all in the created object, that does not lose anything of essential value in translation." Granted Huidobro's sage *caveat*, we are convinced that many of these brief lyrics may be described as "created objects" in the special sense Huidobro meant. They are fascinating objects in themselves.

The Performance

Richard Ford, in his *Gatherings from Spain*, arguably the greatest book about Spain ever written by a non-Spaniard, provides the following evocation of a *flamenco* session which he experienced during his three-year sojourn (1830–1833) on the Peninsula:

> In Spain whenever and wherever the siren sounds are heard, a party is forthwith got up of all ages and sexes, who are attracted by the tinkling like swarming bees. The guitar is part and parcel of the Spaniard and his ballads; he slings it across his shoulder with a ribbon, as was depicted on the tombs of Egypt four thousand years ago. The performers are seldom very scientific musicians; they content themselves with striking the chords, sweeping the whole hand over the strings, or flourishing, and tapping the board with the thumb, at which they are very expert. Occasionally in the towns there is someone who has attained over this ungrateful instrument; but the attempt is a failure. The guitar responds coldly to Italian words and elaborate melody, which never come home to Spanish ears or hearts; for, like the lyre of Anacreon, however often he might change the strings, love, sweet love, is its only theme. The multitude suit the tune to the song, both of which are frequently extemporaneous. They lisp in numbers, not to say verse; but their splendid idiom lends itself to a prodigality of words, whether prose or poetry ... the language comes in aid to the fertile mother-wit of the natives; rhymes are dispensed with at pleasure, or mixed

according to caprice with assonants which consist of the mere recurrence of the same vowels, without reference to that of consonants … a change in intonation, or a few thumps more or less on the board, do the work, supersede all difficulties, and constitute a rude prosody, and lead to music just as gestures do to dancing and to ballads … the sad tunes of these Oriental ditties are still effective in spite of their antiquity; indeed certain sounds have a mysterious aptitude to express certain moods of the mind, in connexion with some unexplained sympathy been the sentient and intellectual organs, and the simplest are by far the most ancient … like the songs of birds, [they] are not taught in orchestras, but by mothers to their infant progeny in the cradling nest.

Ford knew little of the art of the *flamenco*, nothing of its technicalities, but his description is an interesting testimony of the abiding power of the *cantes flamencos*.

A more recent description of a *cante flamenco* performance is to be found (however over-written) in Laurie Lee's *A Rose for Winter* (Penguin, 1955):

The rest of the night was devoted to that most fundamental, most mysterious of all encounters in Andalusian folk-music—the cante flamenco. Three people only take part and the stage itself is reduced to bareness. First comes the guitarist, a neutral, dark-suited figure, carrying his instrument in one hand and a kitchen chair in another. He places the chair in the shadows, sits himself comfortably, leans his cheek close to the guitar and spreads his white fingers over the strings. He strikes a few chords in the darkness, speculatively, warming his hands and his imagination together. Presently the music becomes more confident and free, the crisp strokes of the rhythms more challenging. At that moment the singer walks into the light, stands with closed eyes, and begins to moan in the back of his throat as though testing the muscles of his voice. The audience goes deathly quiet, for what is coming has never been heard before. Suddenly the singer takes a gasp of breath, throws back his head and hits a high barbaric note, a naked wail of sand and desert, serpentine, prehensile. Shuddering then, with contorted and screwed-up face, he moves into the first verse of his song. It is a lament of passion, an animal cry, thrown out, as it were, over burning rocks, a call half-lost in air, imperative and terrible. At first, in this wilderness, he remains alone, writhing in the toils of his words, whipped to more frenzied utterance by the invisible lash of the guitar.

At last, the awful solitude of his cry is answered by a dry shiver of castanets off-stage, the rustle of an awakened cicada, stirred by the man's hot voice. Gradually the pulse grows more staccato, stronger, louder, nearer. Then slow as a creeping fire, her huge eyes smoking, her red dress trailing like flames behind her, the girl appears from the wings. Her white arms are raised like snakes above her, her head is thrown back, her breasts and belly taut, while from her snapping, flickering fingers the black mouths of the castanets hiss and rattle, a tropic tongue, eloquent and savage. The man remains motionless, his arms out stretched, throwing forth loops of song around her and drawing her close to him. And slowly, on drumming feet, she advances, tossing her head and uttering little cries. Once caught within his orbit she begins to circle him, waving and writhing, stamping and turning; her castanets chatter, tremble, whisper; her limbs entangled in his song, coiled in it, reflecting each parched and tortured phrase by the voluptuous postures of her body. And so they act out together long tales of love: singing, dancing, joined but never touching.

Lorca and Cante Jondo

Lorca came early to *cante jondo*. When only twenty, he described himself as "taking down the splendid polyphony of Granadine folksongs." He would also say, "*Cante jondo* seems sometimes like sung prose, destroying all sense of metric rhythm." And again, "The finest degrees of Sorrow and Pain, in the service of the purest, most exact expression, pulse through these brief lyrics often just three or four lines long." He noted that the most striking characteristic of these lyrics is their emotiveness, their undistracted focus on feeling. "It is song without landscape, withdrawn into itself and terrible in the dark."

Lorca's early book, *The Poem of the Deep Song*, is a series of individual lyrics, organised around the traditional form of *cante jondo*, echoing and responding to those lyrics and to their passions.

Here is one of Lorca's lyrics from that book:

> *He was dead there in the street*
> *with a dagger in his chest.*
> *No one knew who he was.*
> *How the lamppost shuddered!*
> *Mother.*
> *How the little lamppost of the street*
> *shuddered!*
> *It was early morning. No one*
> *could look into his eyes*
> *open to the harsh air.*
> *He was dead there in the street*
> *with a dagger in his chest*
> *and no one knew who he was.*
>
> ('Surprise')

Lorca's lyric elaborates the external world of the *cante jondo*, but only to draw attention, explicitly, to the fact that we have no knowledge of the story, the actors, so to speak. In fact, the only actors here are the unknown dead man, the lamppost, the mother who exists only as an isolated word, a wide-eyed "nobody", and, perhaps, as substantial as any of the others, the harsh night air. Here Lorca stands astride that threshold which divides the true intensities of *cante jondo* from the routine versifying of his own time and ours.

There can be no doubt that Lorca learnt a great deal from *cante jondo*. Starting from fundamentals as spare and intense as those of *cante jondo*, Lorca learnt to orchestrate his words to bear a density of texture as taut as that of the full *cante jondo* performance in which words were drawn out across the inflection of the singer's voice, the music of the guitar and the rhythms of the dance. This, of course, is not by any means the whole story of Lorca's great achievement as a poet, but there can be no doubt that some knowledge of *cante jondo* adds significantly to the appreciation of his work. And that is beside their intrinsic beauty and the pleasure they offer.

This Selection

The selection of *cantes flamencos* included in this book is a fairly random one, but we hope it is all the more representative for being just that. As a specific, even formulaic genre is the rule, a good deal of repetition is unavoidable and, we hope, excused on the ground of presenting an over-all view of the vast corpus of the genre. That said, we believe that there are some very beautiful and unique things included in this selection that will encourage the reader to explore further.

Brief Bibliography

Antonio Machado y Álvarez ("Demófilo"): *Cantes flamencos y cantares* (Madrid: Colección Austral, 1998).

Antonio Machado y Álvarez: *Cantes flamencos, recogidos y anotados por Antonio Machado y Álvarez ("Demófilo")* (Barcelona: DVD ediciones, 1998).

Félix Grande: *Memoria del flamenco* (Madrid: Alianza Editorial, 1999).

Federico García Lorca: *Prosa* (Madrid: Alianza Editorial, 1969).

Gypsy Cante, Deep Song of the Caves: Selected and Translated by Will Kirkland (San Francisco: City Lights Books, 1999)

Flamenco Songs

1

The sighs that come from me
and those that come from you,
if they meet on their way
what things they will say!

Suspiros que de mí salgan
y otros que de ti saldrán,
si en el camino se encuentran
¡qué de cosas se dirán!

2

They say absence is
like death, but I say
that's a lie: I adore you
without seeing you.

Dicen que la ausencia es
semejanza de la muerte,
y yo digo que es mentira,
porque te adoro sin verte.

3

How can memory be
the post in absences,
if it brings no messages
nor returns with replies?

¿Cómo ha de ser la memoria
el correo en las ausencias,

si no lleva los recados
ni vuelve con las respuestas?

4

If being fond costed money
you would owe me a lot;
but since it doesn't,
you don't owe me, I owe you not.

Si el querer bien se pagara,
mucho me estabas debiendo;
pero como no se paga,
ni me debes ni te debo.

5

I never ever implore
one that shuns me;
I've got into the habit
of forgetting the oblivious.

En mi vida solicito
al que de mí se retira,
que he tomado por costumbre
olvidar a quien me olvida.

6

With the dolour of not seeing you
I am living here on earth:

if I am not dying,
nobody will from heartbreak.

Con la pena de no verte
estoy viviendo en la tierra:
cuando no me muero yo,
nadie se muere de pena.

7

Your mother is bruiting
something about my honour.
Why cloud the water
she will have to drink?

Anda diciendo tu madre
de mi honra no sé qué:
¿Para qué enturbiar el agua
si la tiene que beber?

8

I must be buried
sitting when I die
so that you can say,
"He's dead but waiting for me."

He de mandar que me entierren
sentado cuando me muera,
para que puedas decir:
—Se murió, pero me espera.

9

Your firm determination,
your praising love so much,
your dying if you couldn't see me,
How quickly you forgot it all!

Aquella firmeza tanta,
y aquel ponderar amor,
y aquel no vivir sin verme,
¡qué pronto se te acabó!

10

I don't know what it is
about the cemetery flowers,
but when the wind rustles them
they seem to be crying.

No sé qué tienen las flores
que están en el camposanto,
que cuando las mueve el viento
parece que están llorando.

11

If for loving another
you want me to die,
have your way:
let me die so another may live.

Si por querer a otro quieres
que yo la muerte reciba,

cúmplase tu voluntad;
muera yo por que otro viva.

12

Grief or no grief
all's grief to me—
yesterday's longing to see you,
today it is the sight of you.

La pena y la que no es pena,
todo es pena para mí;
ayer penaba por verte,
y hoy peno porque te vi.

13

You wanted me to love you,
and I loved you not meaning to;
don't wish for me to loathe you
for I will loathe you indeed.

Quisiste que te quisiera,
y te quise sin querer;
no quieras que te oborrezca,
que te voy a aborrecer.

14

The more you caress me
the more confused I grow

because your caresses are
the prelude to your betrayals.

Mientras más caricias me haces,
más en confusión me pones,
porque tus caricias son
vísperas de tus traiciones.

15

I must punish
the eyes on my face
for looking with affection
at someone who doesn't care.

A los ojos de mi cara
los tengo de castigar,
porque miran con cariño
a quien mal pago les da.

16

I've learned you have someone else.
Don't deny it or excuse yourself;
two lights is the least
that are lit on an altar.

Me han dicho que tienes otra,
no lo niegues ni te excuses,
que lo menos que se encienden
en un altar son dos luces.

17

If blood were sold
you'd be rich and I'd be poor—
you have in your veins
both yours and mine.

Si la sangre se vendiera,
fueras tú rica y yo pobre,
porque tienes en tus venas
la que a mí me corresponde.

18

I wrote it to you crying,
I sent it to you crying.
The tears from my eyes
blurred its sight from me.

Llorando te la escribí,
llorando te la mandé;
las lágrimas de mis ojos
no me la dejaron ver.

19

You said yesterday, Today …
today you're saying, Tomorrow …
and tomorrow you'll say …
I'm no longer in the mood.

Ayer me dijiste que hoy,
hoy me dices que mañana,

y mañana me dirás
que se te quitó la gana.

20

I want to see you burning
in the fire that consumes me
so that you—ingrate—can see
how costly a true love is.

En el fuego en que me abraso
te quisiera ver arder,
para que vieras, ingrata,
lo que cuesta un buen querer.

21

With your soul and your life
you are telling me *Yes,*
but with your thought
you love another more than me.

Con el alma y con la vida
me estás diciendo que sí,
pero con el pensamiento
a otro quieres más que a mí.

22

In a bed of absence
my hope fell ill.

Tears, be patient,
time secures everything.

En una cama de ausencia
cayó mala mi esperanza;
lágrimas, tened paciencia,
que el tiempo todo lo alcanza.

23

My thought
is truly fixed on you:
when I look in the mirror
I see you instead of myself.

Mira tú si yo tendré
fijo en ti mi pensamiento,
que si al espejo me miro,
en vez de verme, te veo.

24

I will unpave the street by your house
and cover it with sand
so I can check the footprints
of those that serenade at your window.

Desempedraré tu calle
y la cubriré de arena,
para mirar las pisadas
de los que rondan tu reja.

25

Seeing you brings me death;
not seeing you makes me live:
I'd sooner see you and die
than live and not see you.

El verte me da la muerte,
y el no verte me da vida;
más quiero morir y verte,
que no verte y tener vida.

26

I am one and you are one:
one and one are two.
Two that should be one.
Ah, if only God willed it so.

Yo soy uno y tú eres una;
uno y una, que son dos;
dos que debieran ser uno;
¡ay, si lo quisiera Dios!

27

If you love me, tell me so;
if not, give me poison.
You will not be the first
to have poisoned her lover.

Si me quieres, dímelo,
y si no dame veneno,

que no serás la primera
que se lo ha dado a su dueño.

28

If my heart is bothering you
throw it in the street.
Let dogs eat it up
if no one wants it.

Si mi corazón te estorba,
anda y échalo a la calle;
que se lo coman los perros,
si es que no lo quiere nadie.

29

These eyes should be blinded
for they see you no more.
Eyes that saw you leaving,
when will they see you return?

Deben cegar estos ojos
que ya no te pueden ver:
¡Ojos que te vieron ir,
cuándo te verán volver!

30

When I see you in agony
there is no happiness in me.

I love you so much
I feel your agony and mine.

Cuando te veo con pena,
en mí no reina alegría,
que como te quiero tanto,
siento la tuya y la mía.

31

I want to speak, but I can't;
and not speaking I speak.
I want and want not to love;
and not meaning to, I do love.

Quiero decir y no digo,
y estoy sin decir diciendo;
quiero y no quiero querer,
y estoy sin querer queriendo.

32

Dish out a different punishment,
one that I can face,
because forgetting you
no longer depends on me.

Échame otra penitencia
que yo la pueda cumplir,
porque llegar a olvidarte
ya no depende de mí.

33

Amorous gazes
are the first messages
that lovers send each other
to say they are in love.

Las miradas amorosas
son los primeros billetes
que se mandan los amantes
para decir que se quieren.

34

How can I forget her
when she was my first love,
and that love takes root
like a plant in the soil?

¿Cómo quieres que la olvide,
si ha sido mi amor primero,
y ese amor echa raíces
como la planta en el suelo?

35

When you love truly
you don't care what people say.
When you have faith in your journey
you never look back.

Cuando se quiere de veras,
no se mira el qué dirán:

quien tiene fe en un camino
no vuelve la cara atrás.

36

I have a pain in my chest
and the doctors tell me
that it is not pain but love
taking root.

Tengo un dolor en el pecho,
y los médicos me dicen
que no es dolor, que es amor
que va criando raíces.

37

I thought that just loving
was a plaything,
and I see now
that one goes through death throes.

Yo pensé que el querer bien
era cosa de juguete,
y ya veo que se pasan
las fatigas de la muerte.

38

Poor me, I complain
of a love that deceived me,

like one looking at a stone
after stumbling over it!

¡Pobre de mí, que me quejo
de un amor que me engañó,
como el que mira la piedra
después que ya tropezó!

39

With or without you
my woes have no cure:
with you, you kill me;
without you, I die.

Ni contigo ni sin ti,
tienen mis males remedio;
contigo, porque me matas;
y sin ti, porque me muero.

40

From my house to yours,
lover, it's barely one step;
from yours to mine,
ah, such a long journey!

Desde mi casa a la tuya,
morena, no hay más que un paso;
desde la tuya a la mía,
¡ay, qué camino tan largo!

41

I love you so much
I'd kill you a hundred times,
and then I'd bring you up
with blood from my veins.

Es tanto lo que te quiero,
que cien veces te matara
y con sangre de mis venas
luego te resucitara.

42

For you I forgot God,
for you I lost renown,
and now I am going to be left
with no God, renown, or you.

Por ti me olvidé de Dios,
por ti la gloria perdí,
y ahora me voy a quedar
sin Dios, sin gloria y sin ti.

43

Every time you go, you tell me:
"Goodbye, I'll see you later."
Since you don't say when,
you always leave me in pain.

Siempre que te vas me dices:
—Adiós, hasta la primera.

Como no me dices cuándo,
siempre me dejas con pena.

44

Here's my heart!
Open it with that key
and you'll see how in here
you are the only one to fit.

Ahí tienes mi corazón;
ábrelo con esa llave,
y verás cómo aquí dentro
sólo tu persona cabe.

45

I love someone who doesn't love me;
that is the point of loving:
a love that's returned
is only self-interest.

Yo quiero a quien no me quiere,
que es la gracia del querer;
que querer a quien nos quiere,
eso es por el interés.

46

The executioner asked my pardon:
I couldn't deny him that.

Justice doesn't pardon,
but criminals will do so.

Perdón me pidió el verdugo,
no se lo quise negar;
la Justicia no perdona,
y perdona el criminal.

47

When I sum up your scorns
and subtract my hopes,
my pains are multiplied
and my soul is divided.

Cuando sumo tus desdenes
y resto mis esperanzas,
se multiplican mis penas
y se divide mi alma.

48

Since loving you
I am in fever;
how can the saying go
that love heals all?

Desde que te estoy queriendo
me están dando calenturas,
y luego dice el refrán
que el amor todo lo cura.

49

I am in agony, in agony,
I can almost say
I am not in agony—
the agony is in me.

Tengo una pena, una pena,
que casi puedo decir
que yo no tengo una pena;
la pena me tiene a mí.

50

Inadvertently, I trod on a flower
that was on his grave;
and from the flower came a sigh
I haven't forgotten since.

Sin querer pisé una flor
que en su sepultura estaba,
y de la flor salió un ¡ay!
que se me clavó en el alma.

51

Because of you I am suffering
more pains and more toils
than the Man Above suffered
when He was down here below.

Estoy pasando por ti
más penas y más trabajos,

que pasó Aquel que está arriba
el tiempo que estuvo abajo.

52

The love I put into you
is a stone thrown into a river;
when it hits the bottom, it's stuck
and won't ever come up.

Es piedra que se echa a un río
el querer que puse en ti;
que llega al fondo, se clava
y ya no vuelve a salir.

53

When I wanted, you wouldn't;
now that you want, I won't.
You'll have a taste of sad love
just as I had it before.

Cuando quise no quisiste,
y ahora que quieres no quiero;
gozarás el amor triste,
cual yo lo gocé primero.

54

In my soul I carry two kisses
which are always with me:

the last one my mother gave me,
and the first one I gave you.

Dos besos tengo en el alma
que no se apartan de mí;
el último de mi madre
y el primero que te di.

55

The handful of flowers
I spill on your grave
are watered by my tears
and so never wither.

Las flores que en su sepulcro
derramo yo a manos llenas
van regadas con mi llanto
y por eso no se secan.

56

Time made a deal
with love,
but whatever love arranges
time spoils.

El tiempo con el amor
hicieron una contrata,
y lo que el amor dispone
el tiempo lo desbarata.

57

Your love is like the bull—
it goes where it's called.
Mine is like the stone:
it stays where it's put.

Es tu querer como el toro,
que donde lo llaman va,
y el mío como la piedra:
donde la ponen se está.

58

Who goes away and comes back
has committed no crime:
the eagle soars up high
and returns to its own place.

El que se retira y vuelve,
no tiene ningún delito;
que el águila se remonta
y vuelve a su mismo sitio.

59

Don't be troubled, my love,
by what happened:
a lost hope
brings a new expectation.

No te apures, compañera,
por aquello que pasó:

una esperanza perdida
trae una nueva ilusión.

60

Whoever buys disappointment
in first loves,
sells disappointment
in second loves.

El que compra un desengaño
en los amores primeros,
en los amores segundos
desengaños va vendiendo.

61

The woman who loves two
is not foolish, but sharp:
if one candle goes out
the other will stay lighted.

La dama que quiere a dos,
no es tonta, que es advertida:
si una vela se le apaga,
otra le queda encendida.

62

The first love I had
made away with my heart:

there's no love like the first;
it makes off with the best.

El primer amor que tuve
se me llevó el corazón:
no hay amor como el primero,
que se lleva lo mejor.

63

On the door of your house
I have written in my blood:
"No debt ever expires
and no debt goes unpaid."

En la puerta de tu casa
tengo escrito con mi sangre:
«No hay plazo que no se cumpla
ni deuda que no se pague».

64

Birdies and I
get up at the same time:
they to serenade the dawn,
I to bemoan my sorrows.

Los pajaritos y yo
nos levantamos a un tiempo;
ellos a cantar el alba,
yo a llorar mi sentimiento.

65

I tell my heart
not to sigh or weep:
however ungrateful you proved to be
many will surely adore it.

A mi corazón le digo
que no suspire ni llore;
que si le has dado mal pago,
no faltará quien le adore.

66

Ah, poor me!
I raise sighs to the air
and the air carries them off
and no one picks them up.

¡Ay, pobrecita de mí,
que doy suspiros al aire,
y el aire se me los lleva,
y no los recoge nadie!

67

If that's what you want, let's switch
our hearts in weeping.
Give me yours and take mine;
let's see which weeps the most.

Si quieres cambiar, cambiemos
corazones a llorar;

dame el tuyo y toma el mío;
veremos cuál llora más.

68

They say that pains kill,
and I say it is not so;
if pains were to kill
I would already be dead.

Dicen que las penas matan,
yo digo que no es así;
que si las penas mataran,
me hubieran matado a mí.

69

They say that voiced troubles
bring consolation:
I told you mine,
but I am dying since.

Los males comunicados
dicen que tienen consuelo;
yo te he contado los míos
y desde entonces me muero.

70

I live alone in the world
and no one remembers me:

I seek shade under trees
and the trees wither.

Vivo solito en el mundo
y de mí nadie se acuerda;
busco en los árboles sombra,
y los árboles se secan.

71

The very eyes of my face,
who wants to buy them?
Beguiling telltales I sell
that expose my grief.

Los ojitos de mi cara,
¿quién me los quiere comprar?
Los vendo por traicioneros,
porque publican mi mal.

72

Cry, cry, eyes of mine!
Cry if you have a reason why.
It is no shame in a man
to cry for a woman.

Llorad, llorad, ojos míos;
llorad si tenéis por qué;
no es vergüenza en un hombre
llorar por una mujer.

73

The love I placed in you,
so strong and so true,
if I had placed it in God
I would have won salvation.

El querer que puse en ti
tan firme y tan verdadero,
si lo hubiera puesto en Dios
hubiera ganado el cielo.

74

Thought, you are killing me,
you are wrecking me.
You are bringing to my mind
things that cannot be.

Pensamiento, tú me matas,
tú me tiras a perder;
tú me traes a la memoria
cosas que no pueden ser.

75

For the pain of an absent one
there is no relief or consolation,
because the harm is near
and the cures are faraway.

Para el dolor de un ausente
no hay alivio ni consuelo,

porque tiene cerca el daño
y distantes los remedios.

76

Whoever wants to know
the colour of pain
should fall in love with a woman
who doesn't love him back.

El que quisiere saber
de qué color es la pena,
de una mujer se enamore
y esta mujer no le quiera.

77

Whoever says that you can be in love
without suffering or enduring
has either always been stupid
or never been truly in love.

Quien diga que ha enamorado
sin sufrir ni padecer,
o siempre ha sido muy necio,
o nunca ha querido bien.

78

You gave me your word
at the edge of the fountain;

since we were by the water
the current carried it away.

La palabra que me diste
a la orilla de la fuente,
como fue cerca del agua
se la llevó la corriente.

79

The flint, being a rock,
when struck by steel
sheds tears of fire.
What of my heart?

La piedra, con ser la piedra,
al golpe del eslabón
echa lágrimas de fuego;
¿qué será mi corazón?

80

Whenever you approach
the orange tree in your patio,
it parts with its flowers
and throws them at your feet.

El naranjo de tu patio,
cuando te acercas a él,
se desprende de sus flores
y te las echa a los pies.

81

Even if I were buried
in the church portico,
should someone say your name
I would raise up my head.

Aunque difunto me hallare
en el compás de la iglesia,
si alguien dijere tu nombre
levantaré la cabeza.

82

The night that thundered so much
I left to meet my girlfriend:
in case the world were to end,
I'd already be close to glory.

La noche que tronó tanto
me fui en busca de mi novia,
por si se acababa el mundo
irme arrimando a la gloria.

83

The toils of love
are the greatest toils—
they are bemoaned singing
though tears are not shed.

Las fatigas del querer
son las fatigas más grandes,

porque se lloran cantando
y las lágrimas no salen.

84

The lover does not boast
but greatly suffers for love.
Love without sorrow or effort
is only love in name.

No ama mucho quien lo dice,
sino quien mucho padece;
que amor sin penas y obras,
de amor sólo el nombre tiene.

85

I have been in Purgatory
and I have seen what suffering is;
and learned that no soul is
condemned for loving greatly.

He estado en el Purgatorio
y he visto lo que son penas,
y sé que por querer bien
ningún alma se condena.

86

When a man who is a real hard man
lets his tears be seen,

down in the depths of his soul
what suffering there must be!

Cuando un hombre que es muy hombre
las lágrimas deja ver,
allá en el fondo del alma
¡qué pena debe tener!

87

To whom will I tell
what is happening to me?
I will tell it to the dirt
when they bury me.

¿A quién le contaré yo
lo que a mí me está pasando?
Se lo contaré a la tierra
cuando me estén enterrando.

88

From that very first instant
when a heart opens its doors,
even if a lover may evade them,
it usually keeps them open.

Desde aquel primer instante
que abre el corazón sus puertas,
aunque las burle un amante,
las suele tener abiertas.

89

Those in love think,
they do, but not clearly;
they think no one's looking
when everyone sees them.

Piensan los enamorados,
piensan, y no piensan bien,
piensan que nadie los mira,
y todo el mundo los ve.

90

Loving words
are the beads of a necklace.
When the first falls off,
all the rest follow.

Las palabras amorosas
son las cuentas de un collar;
en saliendo la primera,
salen todas las demás.

91

He who comes or maybe not,
he who leaves or maybe not,
in love finds
no rival to equal him.

Aquel si viene o no viene,
aquel si sale o no sale,

en los amores no tiene
contento que se le iguale.

92

Two hearts wounded
by the same affliction,
both take their own lives
so not to tell the truth.

Dos corazones heridos
de la misma enfermedad,
ambos se quitan la vida
por no decir la verdad.

93

The eyes of my beloved
gaze at you weirdly;
they kill more in an hour
than death does in a year.

Los ojos de mi morena
tienen un mirar extraño,
que matan en una hora
más que la muerte en un año.

94

Good God!
How painful my trouble!

Sighing I have relief
but I cannot sigh.

¡Válgame Dios de los cielos,
qué penosito es mi mal!
Suspirando tengo alivio,
y no puedo suspirar.

95

They say your hands sting,
but for me they are loving;
though rosebushes sting more
roses are cut from them.

Dicen que espinan tus manos;
para mí son amorosas;
más espinan los rosales
y se le cortan las rosas.

96

The very stars in the sky
and the sands in the sea
resemble my pains:
it takes so long to count them all.

Las estrellitas del cielo
y las arenas del mar,
se parecen a mis penas
en lo largas de contar.

97

You were my first love;
you taught me how to love.
Don't teach me to forget—
I don't want to learn that.

Fuiste mi primer amor,
tú me enseñaste a querer,
no me enseñes a olvidar,
que no lo quiero aprender.

98

I told my secrets to a friend
to see if he would console me;
but my friend was afflicted
by the same illness as myself.

Yo me descubrí a un amigo
por ver si me consolaba,
y el amigo estaba enfermo
del mismo mal que yo estaba.

99

I have no one to weep for me,
nor anyone to suffer for me,
except the very sad bell
that will toll when I die.

No tengo quien por mí llore,
ni quien por mí pase pena,

sino la triste campana
que doble cuando yo muera.

100

Don't tell me to forget you—
you ask me so crying.
You yourself take the advice
so you can come to give me it.

No me digas que te olvide,
que me lo dices llorando;
toma tú misma el consejo
y podrás venir a darlo.

101

If I knew that in the world
hearts were for sale,
I would quickly buy one
for mine is in prison.

Si supiera que en el mundo
se vendían corazones,
fuera yo y comprara uno,
porque el mío está en prisiones.

102

If I call you *sun*, I offend you;
and if *moon*, I am abusing.

And if I call you *bright star*
it seems I am killing you.

Si te digo sol *te ofendo,*
y si luna *te maltrato,*
y si te digo lucero
me parece que te mato.

103

Open my breast and search
its farthest nook—
you will see how you reign
where no woman did.

Ábreme el pecho y registra
hasta el último rincón,
y verás cómo tú reinas
donde ninguna reinó.

104

Loving for loving's sake
without hope of reward
will be a miserable
but true love.

Querer por sólo querer,
sin esperanza de premio,
será un querer desdichado,
pero es querer verdadero.

105

In the house of griefs
I am not welcomed
for I have more griefs
that can fit in there.

En la casa de las penas
ya no me quieren a mí,
porque tengo yo más penas
que las que caben allí.

106

Everyone who meets me
asks me what's wrong:
an illness without cure—
I am forever dying.

Todo el mundo que me ve
me pregunta que qué tengo:
un mal que no tiene cura,
y siempre me estoy muriendo.

107

I'd like to see and not see you;
I'd like to speak and not speak to you;
I wish I didn't know you
so I could forget you.

Quisiera verte y no verte,
quisiera hablarte y no hablarte,

quisiera no conocerte
para poder olvidarte.

108

Every time I pass by and see
where my lover used to live,
I make do with the cage
now that the bird has flown.

Cada vez que paso y miro
donde mi amante vivió,
me contento con la jaula,
que ya el pájaro voló.

109

My heart is riven
with pain and sorrow
on seeing you are alive
but for me you are dead.

El corazón se me parte
de pena y de sentimiento,
al ver que estás en el mundo,
y ya para mí te has muerto.

110

They say we're not in love
because they don't see us talking:

they may ask
your heart and mine.

Dicen que no nos queremos,
porque no nos ven hablar;
a tu corazón y al mío
se lo pueden preguntar.

111

Seeing you, the flowers weep
when you go into your garden,
because the flowers would all like
to look just like you.

Al verte las flores lloran
cuando entras en tu jardín,
porque las flores quisieran
todas parecerse a ti.

112

Withdraw so that people
will not know of our love:
the greater the distance,
the fonder the heart.

Retírate, que la gente
no conozca nuestro amor:
mientras más lejos el santo,
más cerca la devoción.

113

I padlocked my chest
when I saw your beauty
so that no woman can enter it
without your permission.

Eché un candado en mi pecho
desde que vi tu belleza,
porque ninguna entre en él
sin que tú le des licencia.

114

The day you were born
all the flowers bloomed;
and in the baptismal font
the nightingales crooned.

El día que tú naciste
nacieron todas las flores,
y en la pila del bautismo
cantaron los ruiseñores.

115

Take my heart now
and throw it into that fire,
but don't grab the ashes
for they will burn your hand.

Toma allá mi corazón
y échalo en esa candela,

mas no agarres las cenizas,
que te has de quemar con ellas.

116

There are two things in the world
which cannot be forgotten:
the soul's first love
and a mother's affection.

Hay dos cosas en el mundo
que no pueden olvidarse:
el primer amor del alma
y el cariño de una madre.

117

Evils that time carries along,
I wish I'd run through them
so I could apply a cure
before harm comes!

Males que el tiempo acarrea
¡quién pudiera penetrarlos,
para poner el remedio
antes que viniera el daño!

118

What use is to the captive
to have fetters of silver

and chains of gold
if he lacks freedom?

¿De qué le sirve al cautivo
tener los grillos de plata
y las cadenas de oro,
si la libertad le falta?

119

Of the faculties of the soul
memory is the cruellest
because it causes the greatest ill
remembering the greatest good.

De las potencias del alma
la memoria es la cruel,
porque causa el mayor mal
recordando el mayor bien.

120

Time and deception
are two faithful friends:
they wake the sleeping one
and teach the unlearned.

El tiempo y el desengaño
son dos amigos leales,
que despiertan al que duerme
y enseñan al que no sabe.

121

No one in this world should say
"Of this water I will not drink."
However muddy it appears
thirst may force one to.

Nadie diga en este mundo
«de esta agua no beberé»;
por muy turbia que la vea,
le puede apretar la sed.

122

Between true lovers
there is no absence or distance:
thoughts fly between them,
their sighs can be heard.

Entre dos que bien se quieren
no hay ausencia ni distancia,
que los pensamientos vuelan
y los suspiros se alcanzan.

123

On the prison's gate
someone wrote in charcoal:
"Here the good become bad
and the bad become worse."

En la puerta del presidio
hay escrito con carbón:

«Aquí el bueno se hace malo,
y el malo se hace peor».

124

He who overcomes the impossible
wears two equal crowns:
getting his own way
and overcoming difficulties.

El que vence un imposible,
dos coronas tiene iguales:
el salirse con su gusto
y el vencer dificultades.

125

Let no one claim victory
although about to depart;
for many ready to go
were left standing behind.

Ninguno cante victoria
aunque en el estribo esté,
que muchos en el estribo
se suelen quedar a pie.

126

If you hear the death knell,
do not ask who died.

Absent from your sight,
who could it be but me?

Si oyes que tocan a muerto,
no preguntes quién murió,
porque ausente de tu vista,
¿quién puede ser sino yo?

127

Tell me for whom you mourn
so I may mourn too.
It is not right
I'm happy and you're sad.

Dime por quién tienes luto,
para echarlo yo también;
porque tú triste y yo alegre,
eso no parece bien.

128

Ah, me! I've been stolen
of the rose that is mine:
now I see it in other hands
withered and discoloured.

¡Ay de mí, que me han quitado
una rosa siendo mía,
y la veo en otras manos,
marchita y descolorida!

129

If drinking from a fountain
means letting another one dry up,
forgetting in order to love
is a foolish ignorance.

Si por beber de una fuente
has dejado secar otra,
olvidar para querer
es una ignorancia loca.

130

Let the horse race on;
don't pull at the reins.
You'll want it to race some day
but you might not make it do so.

Deja el caballo correr,
no le tires de la rienda,
que pueda ser que algún día
quieras correrlo y no puedas.

131

What benefit to suffer
and shout like a madman
when I am dying for you,
and you are dying for another?

¿De qué me sirve penar
y dar voces como un loco,

si yo me muero por ti
y tú te mueres por otro?

132

My friends despise me
because they see me dejected:
everyone takes advantage
of one's misfortune.

Mis amigos me desprecian
porque me ven abatido:
todo el mundo corta leña
del árbol que está caído.

133

Whoever begins a building work
should finish it
so that no one can ever say
they cowardly gave up.

Aquel que empieza una obra,
razón será que la acabe,
para que nunca se diga
que la dejó por cobarde.

134

A stain fell
on the fine cloth in the shop,

and they sold it cheaper
because it lost its value.

Al paño fino en la tienda
una mancha le cayó,
y se vendió más barato
porque perdió su valor.

135

Since I had not seen her dead
it seemed impossible to me,
and at church I shouted out
but no one answered me.

Como no la vi difunta,
mentira me parecía,
y en la iglesia daba voces
y nadie me respondía.

136

My heart was arrested
and brought to prison,
and it was sentenced to death
though it had committed no crime.

Mi corazón lo prendieron,
y a la cárcel lo llevaron,
y sin delito ninguno
a muerte lo sentenciaron.

137

Damn black clothes
and the tailor who cut them:
my sweetheart is in mourning
though I'm not dead yet!

¡Malhaya la ropa negra
y el sastre que la cortó,
que está mi niña de luto
sin haberme muerto yo!

138

I thought I was the only one
who watered your garden,
but I've noticed there are many
who have some water ready.

Pensaba que era yo solo
el que tu jardín regaba,
mas he visto que son muchos
los que van y sacan agua.

139

Whoever may see me,
will think I am not in pain;
but my heart is black
like a cleaning cloth.

Cualesquiera que me viere,
dirá que no tengo penas,

¡y tengo mi corazón
como la bayeta negra!

140

Last night I dreamt
that two black men killed me;
but it was your two lovely eyes
that were looking at me in anger.

Anoche soñaba yo
que dos negros me mataban,
y eran tus hermosos ojos
que enojados me miraban.

141

If it were not for busybodies
I would dress in mourning,
since my heart
is dead in my chest.

Si no fuera por la gente,
yo me vistiera de luto,
pues tengo mi corazón
dentro del pecho difunto.

142

Your pretty blue eyes,
you stole them from heaven

and to heaven you'll have to account
for the bad you have done with them.

Esos ojitos azules
se los has robado al cielo,
y al cielo le darás cuenta
del mal que hiciste con ellos.

143

Every day it seems to me
I can suffer no more;
and every day you bring me
an increase in sorrow.

Cada día me parece
que no puedo sufrir más,
y cada día me traes
un aumento de pesar.

144

I must have the joiner
make a wooden heart for me
so I don't feel or suffer
nor know what love is.

Un corazón de madera
tengo que mandarme hacer,
que no sienta ni padezca
ni sepa lo que es querer.

145

If I somehow upset you
kill me if you will,
but don't turn your face away
when I meet you in the street.

Si tienes queja de mí,
mátame si te parece,
pero no vuelvas la cara
cuando en la calle te encuentre.

146

Don't look at me or you'll kill me
with those sad eyes of yours;
because to me they stand for
all the badness you did me.

No me mires, que me matas
con esos ojos tan tristes,
porque se me representa
el mal pago que me diste.

147

I am loving you
with the greatest silence,
but you advertise me
like linen-sellers do.

Yo te estoy queriendo a ti
con el más grande silencio,

y tú me vas pregonando
como aquel que vende lienzo.

148

I have already asked you, darling,
more than once
not to knock at that door:
no one will answer you.

Ya te he dicho, corazón,
primera y segunda vez
que no llames a esa puerta,
que no te han de responder.

149

One day I buried my love
thinking it was dead,
and from its dried roots
other plants bloomed.

Yo enterré mi amor un día
creyendo que estaba muerto,
y de sus secas raíces
otras plantas florecieron.

150

The eyes of my lover
are like my troubles:

great like my toils,
black like my burdens.

Los ojos de mi morena
se parecen a mis males:
grandes como mis fatigas,
negros como mis pesares.

151

You will not be the first man
nor I the first woman
who love and forget each other
to love each other again.

No serás tú el primer hombre
ni yo la primera mujer
que se quieran y se olviden
y se vuelvan a querer.

152

I want to be the grave
where they'll bury you
so that I can hold you
for all eternity.

Quisiera ser el sepulcro
donde a ti te han de enterrar,
para tenerte en mis brazos
por toda la eternidad.

153

So great the love you bore me,
your worship of me so grand,
the price at which you set me
and there worthless I stand!

¡Tanto como me querías,
tanto como me adorabas,
tanto como yo valía,
y ahora no valgo nada!

154

Do you remember when you put
your face next to mine,
and crying you told me
that you'd never forget me?

¿Te acuerdas cuando pusiste
tu cara junto a la mía,
y llorando me dijiste
que nunca me olvidarías?

155

Don't strive, my love,
to get some fruit from me:
for the roots dry up
when the water fails the tree.

No te afanes, compañera,
por sacar fruto de mí,

que el árbol que no se riega
se le seca la raíz.

156

My love and your love
are two loves in one,
yet we are always quarelling
about it being mine or yours.

Mi querer y tu querer
son dos quereres en uno,
y siempre estamos riñendo
por si es mío o por si es tuyo.

157

If you despise me for being poor,
I'll say you are right;
a poor man and green wood
burn when set alight.

Si por pobre me desprecias,
digo que tienes razón;
hombre pobre y leña verde
arden cuando hay ocasión.

158

Pity the wretched fellow
who lays his cheek on dirt!

He who remains, in time
will not conceal his zest.

¡Ay, desgraciado de aquel
que pone su cara en tierra!
Que el que queda por acá,
tarde o temprano se alegra.

159

In time you will learn
to know what time is:
bad news is that sometimes
the lesson comes too late.

Con el tiempo aprenderás
a saber lo que es el tiempo:
lo malo es que algunas veces
viene muy tarde el remedio.

160

Kisses and sighs,
tears and complaints:
it's known where they come from,
not how far they go.

Los besos y los suspiros,
las lágrimas y las quejas,
se sabe de dónde salen,
nadie sabe adónde llegan.

161

You say you love me so,
but it's a lie: you fool me;
in so tiny a heart
two souls can't fit.

Dices que me quieres mucho,
y es mentira, que me engañas:
en un corazón tan chico
no pueden caber dos almas.

162

Do not open your heart
to relieve your grief;
for a heart that so opens
is condemned by its speech.

Nadie descubra su pecho
por dar alivio a su pena,
que quien su pecho descubre
por su boca se condena.

163

Don't gossip about anyone—
we all are human flesh,
and there is no wineskin
without some patch on it.

Nadie murmure de nadie,
que somos de carne humana,

y no hay pellejo de aceite
que no tenga su botana.

164

Whoever was never anything
and comes to be something,
wants to be so great a thing
so that there is nothing like him.

Aquel que nunca fue cosa
y que cosa llega a ser,
quiere ser tan grande cosa,
que no hay cosa como él.

165

I agree with the cuckoo,
a bird that never builds a nest;
she lays her eggs in another's nest
and another bird rears her brood.

Soy de la opinión del cuco,
pájaro que nunca anida,
pone el huevo en nido ajeno
y otro pájaro le cría.

166

If you want me to love you
it must be agreed

that you'll look at no one
and I'll look at whomever I please.

Si quieres que yo te quiera,
ha de ser con el ajuste
de que no mires a nadie
y yo mire a quien me guste.

167

I married an old man
to have a warm meal;
but the stove was never lit
and I kept inviting guests.

Yo me casé con un viejo,
por comer algo caliente;
la hornilla estaba apagada
y yo convidando gente.

168

How can you expect me, girl,
to give you all my love
if you are like the weather vane,
here today, there tomorrow.

¿Cómo pretendes, chiquilla,
que ponga mi amor en ti,
si eres como la veleta,
hoy aquí, mañana allí?

169

My father beats me
because I love a grenadier;
and at the sound of the beating, I say,
"Long live fur caps!"

Mi padre me da de palos
porque quiero a un granadero,
y al son de los palos digo:
—¡Vivan las gorras de pelo!

170

Come in, I'm all by myself,
and my mother is in the street;
I'll put out a stool for you:
don't fear—I won't bite.

Entre usté, que estoy solita
y mi madre está en la calle;
le pondré a usté una sillita,
que nadie se come a nadie.

171

I'm dying, I don't know why,
and I don't know what my trouble is;
but I do know when I'll get well
if I-know-who cures me.

Yo me muero no sé cómo,
y mi mal es no sé qué;

yo sanaré bien sé cuándo,
si me cura quien yo sé.

172

You say that you love me so,
that you're dying for me.
Die for me, let me see you,
and then I'll say "I will".

Dices que me quieres mucho
y que te mueres por mí:
muérete, que yo lo vea,
y entonces diré que sí.

173

Don't think that I love you
because I look at your face.
Many go to the fair
to look, but buy nothing.

No pienses que yo te quiero
porque te miro a la cara;
que muchos van a la feria
a ver, y no compran nada.

174

You loved me and I loved you;
you forgot me and I forgot you:

The two of us were to blame:
you first, then myself.

Me quisiste y te quise,
me olvidaste y te olvidé:
los dos tuvimos la culpa,
tú primero y yo después.

175

You're provoking me
to act as a go-between,
and to let the cat out of the bag
so the game is given away.

Tú me estás dando lugar
a que eche la capa al toro,
y que tire de la manta
y que se descubra todo.

176

My girl forgot me,
I couldn't care less:
one shoulder of mutton
drives another one down.

Mi morena me olvidó,
no me da pena maldita,
que la mancha de la mora
con otra verde se quita.

177

Don't think that with caresses
you will smooth me like wax,
I am made of such stuff
that fire itself would freeze me.

Si piensas que con halagos
me has de ablandar como cera,
soy yo de tal calidad,
que el mismo fuego me hiela.

178

You sent me a letter
to say you were forgetting me.
When the news reached me
I no longer remembered you.

Me mandaste a decir
por carta, que me olvidabas:
cuando llegó el parte a mí,
ya de ti no me acordaba.

179

If you die, I'll weep
your absence very much,
but I'll replace you with another
since new things please.

Si te mueres lloraré
por la falta que me haces,

y otro en tu lugar pondré,
que todo lo nuevo place.

180

If your face were a church
and your room were an altar,
and your bed a tomb,
I would bury myself alive.

Si tu cara fuera iglesia,
y tu cuarto fuera altar,
y tu cama sepultura,
vivo me fuera a enterrar.

181

The love of a woman
is like that of a hen:
on missing its own cock
it approaches any other.

El amor de la mujer
es como el de la gallina,
que en faltándole su gallo
a cualquier otro se arrima.

182

Seeing a man and a woman
going out together,

they will sure be held
to be what everyone assumes.

Cuando se ve que van juntos
una mujer con un hombre,
les han de achacar aquello
que cada cual se supone.

183

The first woman God made
deceived father Adam.
If she was made by God,
what of the rest then?

La primera la hizo Dios
y ésa engañó al padre Adán;
cuando a ésa Dios la hizo,
¿cómo serán las demás?

184

Disdainful women
are like olives:
the greener they look,
the riper they are.

Las mujeres desdeñosas
son como las aceitunas:
la que parece más verde
suele ser la más madura.

185

I don't want to love a maiden.
A married woman told me
that it is only robbers
who open a closed coffer.

No quiero amor con doncella,
que me ha dicho una casada
que es oficio de ladrones
abrir un arca cerrada.

186

Make me some shoes
with very high heels;
I am a small girl and can't
reach my lover's arms.

Hágame usté unos zapatos
con el tacón que levante,
que soy chiquita y no alcanzo
a los brazos de mi amante.

187

I want to see you
thirty days a month,
seven days a week,
every minute once.

Yo quisiera estarte viendo
treinta días cada mes,

siete días en semana,
cada minuto una vez.

188

The love of a poor man
is like that of a dwarf cock;
it spends all year long
trying but getting nowhere.

El amor del hombre pobre
es como el del gallo enano,
que en querer y no alcanzar
se le pasa todo el año.

189

The eyes of a widow
advertise along the street:
"This room is for rent
for no one lives here."

Los ojos de la viüda
van diciendo por la calle:
—Esta habitación se alquila,
porque no la habita nadie.

190

A lover is like a child
who, angry, scraps his food;

once given affection
he eats it and asks for more.

El amante es como el niño
que se enoja y tira el pan,
y en haciéndole un cariño,
se lo come y pide más.

191

A woman and a coin
are very much the same:
some look like they are gold
and turn out to be false.

La mujer y la moneda
tienen mucha semejanza:
algunas de oro parecen,
y resulta que son falsas.

192

Loving one woman is nothing,
loving two is falseness,
loving three and deceiving four ...
that is a Godgiven gift.

Querer una no es ninguna,
querer dos es falsedad,
querer tres y engañar cuatro ...
eso es gracia que Dios da.

193

I ate the heart
of a romaine lettuce.
Let others eat the leaves.
What do I care?

De la lechuga romana
el cogollo me comí;
que otros se coman las hojas,
¿qué cuidado me da a mí?

194

My wife's mother
loves me so much …
affection so blinds her
she can't stand the sight of me.

Es tanto lo que me quiere
la madre de mi mujer,
tanto le ciega el cariño …
que no me puede ni ver.

195

A newlywed old man
kept close watch on his vineyard,
and he just gathered the gleanings
when he harvested his grapes.

Un viejo recién casado
guardaba mucho su viña,

y se halló con el rebusco
cuando fue a hacer la vendimia.

196

Whoever trusts women
knows very little of the world.
It's like relying on doors
for which everyone has the keys.

Quien se fía de mujeres
muy poco del mundo sabe,
que se fía de unas puertas
de que todos tienen llaves.

197

Twelve hens and one cock
almost always are content;
one woman and one man
almost never.

Doce gallinas y un gallo
casi siempre están conformes,
y casi nunca lo está
una mujer con un hombre.

198

If any of you wants to send
their regards to hell

don't miss the chance:
my mother-in-law's about to die.

El que quisiere mandar
memorias a los infiernos,
la ocasión la pintan calva:
mi suegra se está muriendo.

199

Some place or other,
there is some saint or other;
saying some prayer or other
brings you some gain or other.

En un lugar, no sé dónde,
hay un yo no sé qué santo;
rezándole un no sé qué,
se gana yo no sé cuánto.

200

I want no married woman's love.
A widow once told me this:
out on the street they'll strip bare
him who wears someone else's clothes.

No quiero amor con casada,
que me ha dicho una viuda
que a quien de ajeno se viste
en la calle lo desnudan.

201

Don't ever fall in love
with a lad who never courted;
for he who didn't court when young
will court later when married.

En tu vida te enamores
de mozo que no ha rondado;
que el que no ronda de mozo,
ronda después de casado.

202

I'd sooner stay in a ring
as a fighting bull charges
than wait for a woman saying:
"What do I care?"

Más quisiera en una plaza
a un toro bravo esperar,
que no a una mujer que diga:
—¿Qué cuidado se me da?

203

A woman's love
is like that of a dog:
however much it's beaten
it never leaves its master.

El amor de las mujeres
suele ser como el del perro,

que aunque le sacudan palos,
nunca desampara al dueño.

204

God made a woman
out of the rib of Adam
to leave men
a tough bone to crack.

De una costilla de Adán
hizo Dios a la mujer,
para dejarle a los hombres
ese hueso que roer.

205

If only I found myself with you
and the door were locked;
if only the locksmith died
and the key just broke!

¡Si yo me viera contigo
con la llavecita echada,
y el herrero se muriera,
y la llave se quebrara! ...

206

The shoes I throw out
and fling on the trash heap;

if another puts them on,
what do I care?

Zapatos que yo desecho
y los tiro al muladar,
si otro llega y se los pone,
¿qué cuidado se me da?

207

According to women
men are the devil,
yet they are forever wanting
to see red and go to hell.

Los hombres son el demonio,
según dicen las mujeres,
y siempre están deseando
que el demonio se las lleve.

208

I did not ask for you;
remember, you looked for me,
then you went off at your pleasure
and returned without being called.

Yo no te solicité;
recuerda que me buscaste,
te marchaste por tu gusto
y volviste sin llamarte.

209

If women ever had
the freedom of men,
they would waylay people
to steal their hearts.

Si las mujeres tuvieran
la libertad de los hombres,
salieran a los caminos
a robar los corazones.

210

The woman who breaks her plate
before it is mealtime,
however pretty she is,
will never find a spouse.

La dama que rompe el plato
sin ser hora de comer,
por muy bonita que sea,
nunca encuentra mercader.

211

Even the timbers on the mountain
are different from each other:
some are good for carving saints,
some just for making coal.

Hasta la leña en el monte
tiene su separación:

una sirve para santos,
y otra para hacer carbón.

212

Love hidden
   in silence
wreaks havoc
   in the breast:
   its flames
with no way out
   burn up the soul.

El amor que se oculta
   bajo el silencio,
hace mayor estrago
   dentro del pecho.
   Porque sus llamas,
como no hallan salida,
   queman el alma.

213

In a green meadow
I laid out my shawl;
three roses appeared, Mother,
like three bright stars.

En un prao berde
tendí mi pañuelo;
cómo salieron, mare, tres rositas
como tres luseros.

214

Dear Mother of my soul,
dear Father, what a shame
our people found out
my oven is for sale.

Mare mía de mi alma,
pare mío, qué vergüenza,
que s'enteren los gitanos
que tengo la fragua en venta.

215

I am not who I was
nor what I used to be;
I'm a sad piece of furniture
put against the wall.

Yo ya no soy el que era
ni quien solía yo ser,
soy un mueble de tristeza
arrumbaíto a la paré.

216

In other times gypsies
wore socks of silk
but now unfortunately
they wear shackles and chains.

Otras veces los gitanos
gastaban medias de seda

y ahora por su desgracia
gastan grillos y caenas.

217

If my mother could see me
she would not know me
with this jacket on my shoulder
and these chains on my feet.

Si me viera a mí mi mare
no me había de conosé,
con la chaquetita al hombro
y la caenita ar pie.

218

I am in a prison
full of horrors;
they bring me up and down
to take my statement.

Estoy en un calaboso
lleno de abominaciones,
ya me suben, ya me bajan
a tomar declaraciones.

219

They jail the beggar,
they arrest the robber,

but who doesn't beg or steal
dies of hunger in a corner.

Al que mendiga lo encierran
y meten preso al ladrón,
el que no pide ni roba
muere de hambre en un rincón.

220

Why are you beating me so,
what harm have I done?
I just fell asleep—
sleep overcomes the lion.

A qué pegarme estos palos,
qué daño t'he jecho yo.
Que m'he quedaíto dormío
y el sueño rinde al león.

221

The laments of a captive
cannot reach his homeland,
for the sea lies in between
and they drown in the water.

Los lamentos d'un cautivo
no pueden llegar a España
porque está la mar por medio
y s'ajogan en el agua.

222

My hands on the oar,
my feet on the rudder;
no one sails the world
with more toils than me.

Llevo las mano en el remo
y los pies en el timón,
no hay quien navegue en er mundo
con más fatigas que yo.

223

The gypsies of El Puerto
were the most unfortunate—
they were sentenced
to work the mercury mines.

Los gitanitos del Puerto
fueron los más desgraciaos
que a las minas del azogue
se los llevan sentenciaos.

224

The gypsies of El Puerto
and those, too, of Jerez.
Fortunate the eyes
that have yet to see them.

Los gitanitos del Puerto
y también los de Jerez.

Dichosos serán los ojos
que los golverán a ver.

225

What I see in you, woman,
is rare among our kind;
the sorrows you suffer
don't show on your face.

They don't show on my face
though my heart feels them;
I don't show my sorrows
for fear of gossiping.

For fear of gossiping
I don't show my sorrows;
but time will tell
how much I loved you.

Lo que se be en ti, mujé,
no s'ha bisto entre jitanas,
que las fatigas que tienes
no te salen a la cara.

No me salen a la cara
y mi corazón lo siente;
no publico mis fatigas
por er desí de la jente.

Por er desí de la jente
no publico mis fatigas;
con er tiempo se sabrá
lo mucho que te quería.

226

They took me from that prison
and put me in a much worse place;
there I couldn't even see
my own fingers or my hands.

A mí me sacaron del calaboso
y me metieron en otro más malo
que allí ya no podía ni verme
ni los deítos de las manos.

227

When I was in prison
I used to amuse myself
counting the links
of my chains.

Cuando yo estaba en prisiones
solito me divertía
en contar los eslabones
que mi caena tenía.

228

For three days I have eaten
nothing but tears and bread.
This is all the food
my guards give me.

Ya van tres días que no como
más que lágrimas y pan.

Éstos son los alimentos
que mis guardianes me dan.

229

My clothes are for sale.
Who wants to buy them?
I am selling them cheap
to buy your freedom.

Mi ropa 'stá en venta,
quién la quié mercá,
que la vendo por poco dinero
pa tu libertá.

230

Here they come for inspection,
I can hear the keys jangling,
as my poor heart weeps
droplets of blood.

Ya viene la requisa,
ya suenan las llaves,
cómo me llora mi corazonito
gotitas de sangre.

231

I am asking from the moon
that is high in the sky;

I am asking it to free my father
from his prison.

A la luna le pido,
la del alto sielo,
como le pido que saque a mi pare
de 'onde está preso.

232

Right honourable judge
and other gentlefolk:
these hardships to my body
are not fit and proper.

Señor alcalde mayor
y demás señores:
estas fatigas a este cuerpo mío
no le corresponden.

233

What is all that shouting
that is coming to me?
I bet it is my mother's
looking for me.

Qué voces son esas
que a mí m'están dando,
si serán las voces de la mare mía
que m'está buscando.

234

The doors were opened
and a voice could be heard.
Then they began the trial
to sentence him.

S'abrieron las puertas
y sonó una voz,
ya principiaron la pública audencia
que lo condenó.

235

We heard the death knell
of San Juan de Dios's bells
as they killed Torrijo the brave.
It's such a great shame!

Doblaron campanas
de San Juan de Dios
como mataron a Torrijo el valiente,
¡miren qué doló!

236

The day they put Riego
under sentence of death,
the sighs of his men
reached up to heaven.

El día que en capilla
metieron a Riego

los suspiritos que daban sus tropas
llegaban ar sielo.

237

My dearest Curro,
tell my mother
how I am in this doorway
struck down in blood.

Comparito mío Curro,
dígale a mi mare
cómo me queo en esta casapuerta
revolcao en sangre.

238

When I lie dead
this errand I ask from you:
my hands to be bound
with the lace of your black hair.

Cuando yo me muera
mira que te encargo
que con la sinta e tu pelo negro
m'amarren las manos.

239

Here, there and everywhere
they call me the madman;

the one to blame for my ills
I know all too well.

Por esos munditos
me yaman er loco;
ar que tiene la culpa e mis males
yo bien lo conosco.

240

Dear love of mine,
see how by loving you
I am despised
by all of my people.

Compañera mía,
mira por quererte,
cómo me veo aborresiíto
de toíta mi gente.

241

I am not from around
nor was I born here:
fate, turning and turning,
has brought me here.

No soy de esta tierra
ni en enya nasí:
la fortuniya, roando, roando,
m'ha traío hasta aquí.

242

Dear sister of mine,
what a fine woman!
Of the bit of bread she had
she offered me half.

Hermaniya mía,
¡qué güena gitana!
De un peasito e pan que tenía
la mitá me daba.

243

Don't be jealous,
don't be worried,
sweetheart; I could love no one
while you are alive.

No tengas selitos
ni pases fatigas,
compañera mía, que no quiero a naide
mientras tú me bibas.

244

I climbed the wall;
the wind answered me.
Why so many sighs
if nothing can be done?

Subí a la muraya
me respondió er biento:

¿Pa qué bienen tantos suspiritos
si ya no hay remedio?

245

I looked out the door
to see if she was coming,
my soul's sweetheart,
and she'd found her way.

M'asomé a la puerta
por be si benía
la compañera mía e las mis entrañas,
e buscá la bía.

246

Tell me who you hang around with
and I'll tell you who you are;
since you hang around with wicked people
you yourself are wicked.

Ime con quién andas
te iré quién eres;
como tú anda con malas personas,
malito tú eres.

247

Dear Mother,
I don't know where

the silver of the mirror
I was looking in has gone.

Maresita mía,
yo no sé por dónde
al espejito donde me miraba
se le fue el asogue.

248

To see you in the past
I would have paid;
now not to see you, girl,
I turn my face away.

Un día por berte,
dinero yo daba;
compañerita, ahora por no berte
güerbo yo la cara.

249

I'm calling death,
but it won't come to me;
even death, sweetheart,
has pity on me.

A la muerte yamo,
no quiere bení;
que hasta la muerte tiene, compañera,
lástima e mí.

250

With the coming of day
my torments arrive;
but saying my prayers
gives me back my breath.

Ar venir er día
yegan mis tormentos;
pero en yegando a las orasiones
recobro el aliento.

251

I don't wish to remember
things of the past;
my poor heart is weeping
droplets of blood.

De cosas pasáas
no quiero yo acordarme;
porque me yora mi corasonito
gotitas e sangre.

252

Let the bells toll,
toll with pain:
the love of my heart
is dead.

Doblen las campanas,
doblen con doló;

que s'ha muerto la mi compañera
e mi corasón.

253

The anvil and hammer
break metals;
nothing will break
the vow I made to you.

Er yunque y martiyo
rompen los metales;
er juramento que yo a ti t'he jecho
no lo rompe naide.

www.ingramcontent.com/pod-product-compliance
Lightning Source LLC
Chambersburg PA
CBHW022155080426
42734CB00006B/447